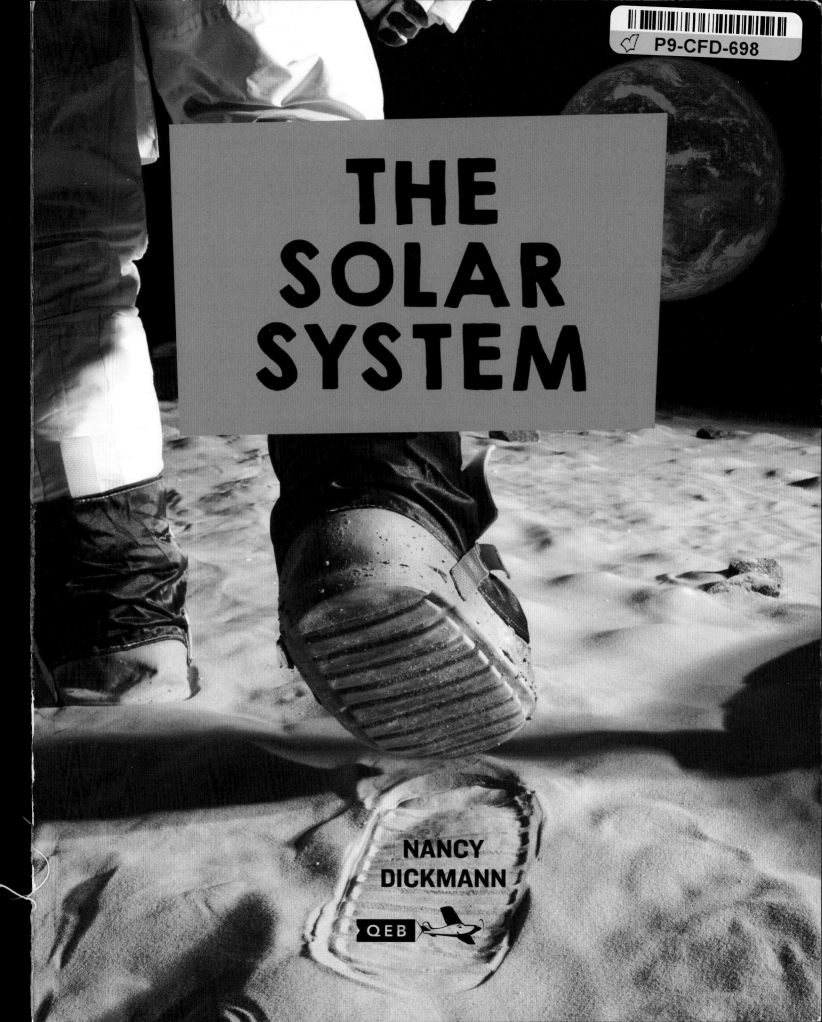

THE SOLAR SYSTEM

NANCY
DICKMANN

QEB

Written by Nancy Dickmann
Edited and Designed by Calcium Creative
Publisher: Maxime Boucknooghe
Editorial Director: Victoria Garrard

First published in the United States by
QEB Publishing, Inc.
6 Orchard
Lake Forest
CA 92630

www.qed-publishing.co.uk

A CIP record for this book is available from the Library of Congress.

ISBN 978 1 60992 985 5

Printed in China

Picture Credits:
Alamy 4–5 Dimitar Todorov, 12cl Susan E. Degginger, 23cl NG Images, 25tr blickwinkel, 51tr North Wind Picture Archives, 52–53 Gunter Hofer.

ESA 33br ESA/DLR/FU Berlin/Bill Dunford, 70–71 J.Huart, 71cr ESA/Rosetta/MPS for OSIRIS Team MPS/UPD/LAM/IAA/SSO/INTA/UPM/DASP/IDA.

Getty Images fc fStop Images - Caspar Benson, 6–7 Darrell Wyatt, 6br Christian Miller, 7cr Jeffrey Conley, 12–13 gucchi, 14–15 Ivo Peer/EyeEm,
16–17 fStop Images - Caspar Benson, 30–31 Sergey Goshkov, 40–41 Science and Society Picture Library, 50–51 UniversalImagesGroup,
66–67 Dan Macmillan www.Catching Magic.Com, 72–73 Tony Hallas.

NASA 3br NASA/Johns Hopkins University Applied Physics Laboratory/Carnegie Institution of Washington, 8–9 NASA, 10–11 SDO/AIA/Goddard Space Flight
Center, 10bl SDO/HMI, 11bl Hinode JAXA/NASA/PPARC, 13br NASA, 17tl NASA/SAIC/Pat Rawlings, 17bl NASA/MSFC, 20–21 NASA/Johns Hopkins University
Applied Physics Laboratory/Carnegie Institution of Washington, 21tr NASA/Johns Hopkins University Applied Physics Laboratory/Carnegie Institution of
Washington, 22–23 NASA/Johns Hopkins University Applied Physics Laboratory/Carnegie Institution of Washington, 26–27 NASA/JPL, 27tr USSR/NASA
National Space Science Data Centre, 34–35 NASA/JPL-Caltech, 35br NASA/JPL/Cornell, 36–37 NASA/JPL-Caltech/MSSS, 37tr NASA/JPL, 38–39 NASA/JPL/
Space Science Institute, 41cr NASA, 41bl NASA/JPL, 42–43 NASA, 43br NASA/JPL-Caltech/SETI Institute, 44–45 NASA/JPL, 45tr NASA/JPL-Caltech/Space
Science Institute, 47tr NASA, 49br NASA/JPL/Space Science Institute, 53br NASA, 54–55 NASA/JPL, 55br NASA, 56–57 NASA/JPL, 57tr NASA, 57br NASA,
59tr NASA/JPL-Caltech/UCLA/MPS/DLR/IDA/PSI, 60–61 NASA/Johns Hopkins University Applied Physics Laboratory/Southwest Research Institute, 60c
NASA/JHUAPL/SWRI, 61br NASA, 63tr NASA, 64–65 NASA/JPL-Caltech/UCLA/MPS/DLR/IDA, 65cr NASA/JPL-Caltech/UCLA/MPS/DLR/IDA, 79 NASA.

REX Shutterstock 72cl ZUMA.

Science Photo Library 5tr Luis Argerich, 24–25 NASA, 32–33 Joe Tucciarone, 39tr Detlev van Ravenswaay, 46–47 Chris Butler, 48–49 Science Photo Library,
58–59 Mark Garlick, 68–69 Walter Pacholka, Astropics, 69cr Julian Baum, 74–75 Edward Kinsman, 76–77 Carlos Clarivan.

Shutterstock 3b/g Tjeffersion, 9cr Dmitry Kosterev, 15c Procy, 18–19 AstroStar, 18–19b/g Grisha Bruev, 19t Designua, 20bl Damiano Mariotti, 28–29 Triff,
29tl Pierre Leclerc, 29cr Action Sports Photography, 31cr Mopic, 44bl MarcelClemens, 50bl Tristan3D, 62–63 Andrea Danti, 75br Galyna Andrushko,
77bl Martin Capek, 77tr Sung Choi.

Wikipedia 66tc.

CONTENTS

OUR SOLAR SYSTEM

Our home **planet**, Earth, is part of a larger group of planets. It's called the **solar system** and is made up of the Sun and everything that **orbits**, or circles, it. This includes the planets and their **moons**.

JUPITER

MERCURY

EARTH

VENUS

MARS

EARTH'S MOON

NOT JUST PLANETS

Our solar system has eight planets and at least 146 moons—more are being discovered every year! But there are also other objects, such as **asteroids**, **comets**, and **dwarf planets**.

The Sun is at the center of the solar system.

JUPITER

MOON ···· ▶

VENUS

Jupiter, Venus, and the Moon shine because they reflect light from the Sun.

URANUS

SATURN

NEPTUNE

WAY BACK WHEN

The Sun and the rest of the solar system were formed billions of years ago. They were made when clouds of gas and dust started clumping together. Eventually the clumps became big enough to form planets and other objects.

THE SUN

The Sun is just one of billions of **stars** in the universe. It looks huge compared to the other stars in the sky, but that is because it is so much closer to us. Even so, it is about 93 million miles (150 million kilometers) away!

WATCH YOUR STEP

You couldn't stand on the surface of the Sun. Stars do not have a solid surface, like Earth does. All stars are giant balls of hot, glowing plasma, which is like a gas.

STAR FACT!

Stars can be different colors. Really big, hot stars are often blue, and smaller, cooler stars are often orange or red.

The Sun seems huge, but it is just an average-sized star.

WE NEED THE SUN

All life on Earth depends on the Sun. We use its light to see, and its heat keeps us warm. The Sun is incredibly hot, but it is also so far away that by the time its **energy** reaches us, it has cooled down a lot.

Plants use light energy from the Sun to make the food that helps them grow.

INSIDE THE SUN

All stars produce heat and light. This happens deep inside, in an incredibly hot place called the **core**. In the core, tiny pieces of **matter** called **atoms crash together**. This releases energy.

CONVECTION ZONE

RADIATIVE ZONE

CORE

STAR FACT!

At the center of the Sun, temperatures can reach 27 million degrees Fahrenheit (15 million degrees Celsius)!

WHAT A BLAST!

The way that the Sun releases energy means that it is constantly exploding. Luckily, the Sun is so huge that the explosion won't run out of fuel for several billion years.

The Sun is made up of several different layers. Some are hotter than others.

SUNSPOTS
(see pages 10-11)

CORONA

RELEASING ENERGY

Once the energy is produced, it moves up from the core, through the radiative zone and convection zone, to the surface. This can take many thousands of years. It finally gets to the surface of the Sun and is released into space. It takes about eight minutes for light energy from the Sun to reach Earth.

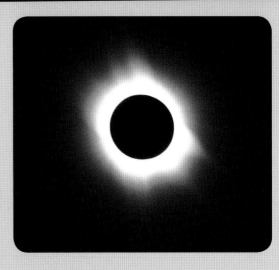

The corona is the outer part of the Sun's **atmosphere**. It is hard to see unless the Sun is blocked out.

SUNSPOTS AND SOLAR FLARES

The Sun's surface changes all the time. Sometimes dark spots called "sunspots" appear. These spots are cooler than the rest of the Sun's surface. They last for a while before disappearing.

DARK SPOTS

People used to think that sunspots were caused by planets passing in front of the Sun. Now we know that they are caused by the Sun's magnetism.

A coronal mass ejection can be bigger than the Sun itself.

A sunspot can last for anywhere from a few days to a few weeks.

SOLAR EXPLOSIONS

Sometimes there are explosions on the surface of the Sun. Sections of the Sun's matter get heated up really quickly and release huge amounts of energy. This is called a solar flare. Even bigger explosions, called **coronal mass ejections**, can also happen.

The Sun's surface has a grainy look, caused by bubbles of hot and cold gas inside.

ECLIPSE!

The Moon travels around Earth, and sometimes it passes between Earth and the Sun for a few minutes. When this happens, the Moon blocks the Sun from view and an eclipse takes place.

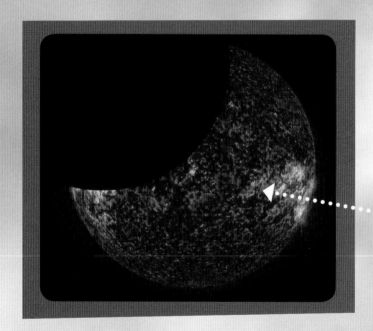

When an eclipse begins, it looks like the Moon is taking a bite out of the Sun.

STAR FACT!

When Earth is between the Sun and the Moon, Earth's shadow can cause a lunar eclipse. This makes the full Moon seem to disappear.

DAYTIME DARKNESS

During an eclipse, the Moon blocks out the Sun's light for a few minutes. The skies grow dark, and the temperature drops. Then the Moon moves away, and the Sun reappears. An eclipse is only visible from a small part of Earth's surface.

JUST RIGHT

The Sun is about 400 times bigger than the Moon, but it is also about 400 times farther away from Earth. This means that the two objects appear to be about the same size in the sky—perfect for eclipses!

When the Moon is at its farthest point from Earth, it doesn't appear big enough to cover the Sun completely. This leads to a ring-shaped eclipse.

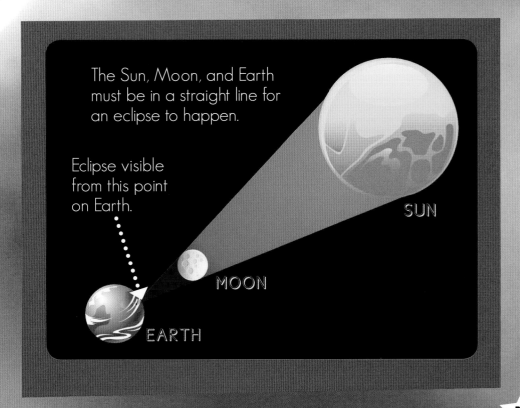

The Sun, Moon, and Earth must be in a straight line for an eclipse to happen.

Eclipse visible from this point on Earth.

SUN

MOON

EARTH

THE MOON

The Moon is a round, hard, rocky ball. It is smaller than Earth—in fact, nearly four Moons could fit across Earth's diameter. It takes about 29 days for the Moon to travel around Earth.

Once a month, the Moon appears as a complete circle in the sky. Our months are based on the time from one of these full moons to the next.

MOONLIGHT

The Moon is the brightest object in the night sky, but it does not make its own light. Instead, its pale-colored rocks reflect the Sun's light.

14

ON THE SURFACE

From Earth, we always see the same side of the Moon. It has a mixture of **craters**, mountains, and dark plains. Spacecraft have taken photographs of the far side of the Moon. It has more craters and fewer dark areas.

Craters form when space objects crash into the Moon. On Earth, our thick atmosphere protects us from many impacts, and the weather can wear away craters. The Moon has no atmosphere, so it has more craters.

STAR FACT!

The Moon's biggest crater is 1,500 miles (2,414 kilometers) across and over 5 miles (8 kilometers) deep!

MOON EXPLORATION

The Moon is the only place in the solar system where we have sent astronauts. Twelve different men have walked on the Moon. We have also sent robot **rovers** and spacecraft to study the Moon.

STAR FACT!

Gravity on the Moon is weak. On the Moon, it would feel like you weighed about one-sixth of what you do on Earth. The astronauts bounced around in the weak gravity.

FIRST LANDING

The first astronauts to land on the moon arrived on July 20, 1969. When Neil Armstrong stepped off the ladder onto the Moon's surface, he said, "That's one small step for man, one giant leap for mankind."

Neil Armstrong described the Moon's surface as being "fine and powdery." His boots left clear footprints.

MOON SCIENCE

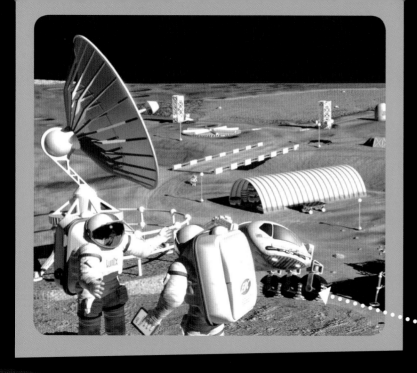

The astronauts weren't just having an exotic vacation. They collected samples of Moon rocks and set up science experiments. They discovered new information about the Moon's surface, structure, and **magnetic field**.

Many people believe that one day we will set up colonies on the Moon.

In 1971, this "moon buggy" drove across the Moon's surface at about 8 miles (13 kilometers) per hour.

GROWING AND SHRINKING

The Moon seems to change shape. It grows from a thin crescent to a full circle, and then shrinks back to a crescent again. But how can part of the Moon just disappear?

WANING GIBBOUS

REFLECTING LIGHT

The Moon reflects the Sun's light, so only the half of the Moon that is facing the Sun shines brightly—the other side is dark. Depending on where it is in its orbit around Earth, we might see only part of its bright side.

FULL MOON

STAR FACT!

When Earth is between the Moon and the Sun, we see the whole bright side. When the Moon is between Earth and the Sun, its bright side is facing away from us, and we can't see it.

This image shows just a few of the phases that the Moon goes through over a month.

THIRD QUARTER

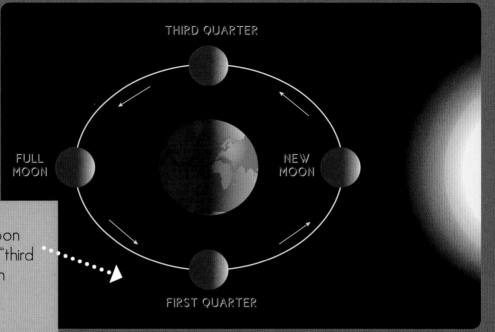

THIRD QUARTER

FULL MOON

NEW MOON

FIRST QUARTER

From Earth, when the Moon is in its "first quarter" and "third quarter" positions, we can see half of its bright side and half of its dark side.

PHASES OF THE MOON

We give different names to the shapes of the Moon in the sky. When we see the whole circle, it's called a full moon. When only a tiny sliver is visible, it's called a crescent moon.

CRESCENT MOON

FIRST QUARTER

WAXING GIBBOUS

MERCURY

The planets **closest to the Sun are small and rocky. Mercury is the smallest planet, and is the closest one to the Sun. Its rocky surface is covered with craters, as well as mountains, plains, and valleys.**

HOT AND COLD

Since Mercury is so close to the Sun, it can get incredibly hot: up to 801 degrees Fahrenheit (427 degrees Celsius) during the day. Those temperatures would melt lead! At night, it gets down to a supercold -290 degrees Fahrenheit (-179 degrees Celsius).

Mercury is just over 3,000 miles (4,828 kilometers) wide. Earth is about two and a half times as wide.

Mercury was named after the Roman messenger god, because it moved so quickly through the sky.

SPEEDY PLANET

Mercury travels through space much faster than Earth does: about 106,000 miles (171,000 kilometers) per hour. It takes Mercury just under 88 days to travel around the Sun.

The *Mercury Messenger* spacecraft orbited Mercury from 2011 until 2015, when it crashed into the planet's surface.

STAR FACT!

Mercury used to have active **volcanoes**. Instead of being tall mountains, like volcanoes on Earth, they were vents down on the surface, where **lava** used to flow out.

CRATERS EVERYWHERE!

Mercury has more craters than any other planet. On planets like Earth and Venus, the thick atmosphere can make space rocks break apart or burn up before they hit the surface. Mercury's extremely thin atmosphere does not stop space rocks from hitting its surface.

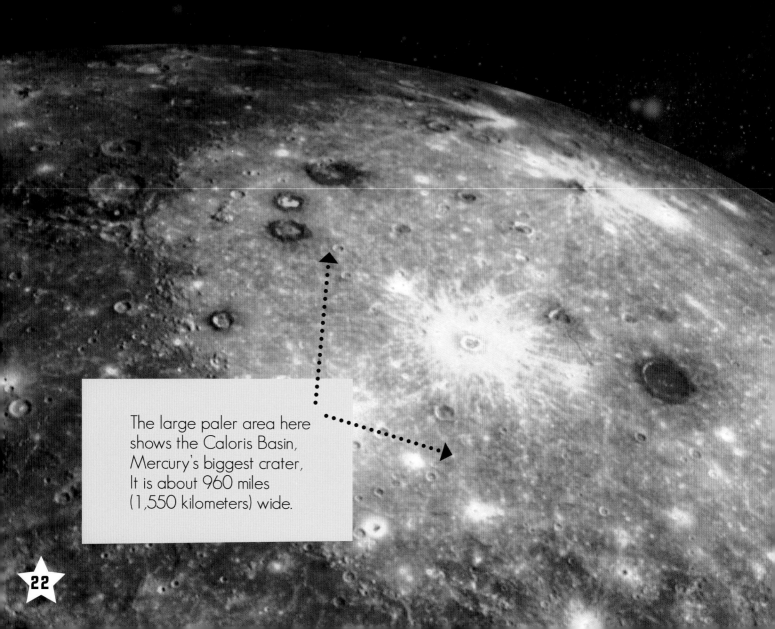

The large paler area here shows the Caloris Basin, Mercury's biggest crater. It is about 960 miles (1,550 kilometers) wide.

WEARING AWAY

On Earth, wind and running water wear away the rocks that form many craters. Lava from volcanic eruptions can cover up craters with new rock. But on Mercury, craters can last for many millions of years.

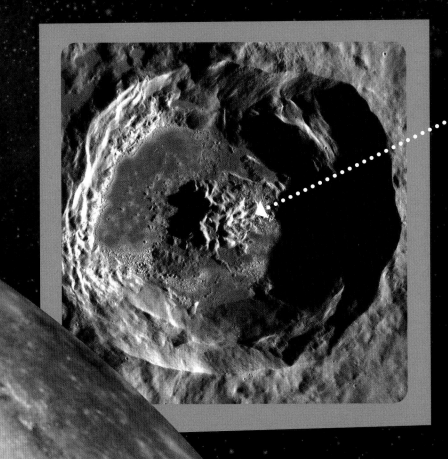

Some large craters have mountains in the middle. These are caused by the force of the rock "springing back" after the impact.

WEIRD SURFACE

Mercury's surface has some folds of rock that look like wrinkles. Scientists think that a long time ago, the planet cooled down and shrank, making the outer crust wrinkle up.

23

VENUS

The second planet from the Sun is Venus. You've probably seen it in the night sky. After the Sun and Moon, it is the brightest space object that we can see.

Venus's thick clouds stop us from seeing its surface through a **telescope**.

TWIN SISTER?

Venus is sometimes called "Earth's twin." The two planets are almost the same size, and they have about the same **mass** as well. They are also made of the same types of rocks. But Venus doesn't have water, like Earth does.

Venus (top left) is often most visible at dusk and dawn, so it is sometimes called "the morning star" or "the evening star."

LAND OF VOLCANOES

Venus's surface is mostly made of smooth plains, but it also has some volcanoes. Compared to volcanoes on Earth, they are enormous! More than 150 of them are at least 60 miles (97 kilometers) across.

STAR FACT!

Venus is fairly close to Earth, but that's not the only reason it looks so bright. Its thick clouds reflect a lot of sunlight.

THE DEADLY PLANET

Venus looks beautiful, but it's not a place you would want to visit! Even though it's our closest neighbor in space, we will probably never send astronauts there. Below the swirling clouds lies a hot and dangerous world.

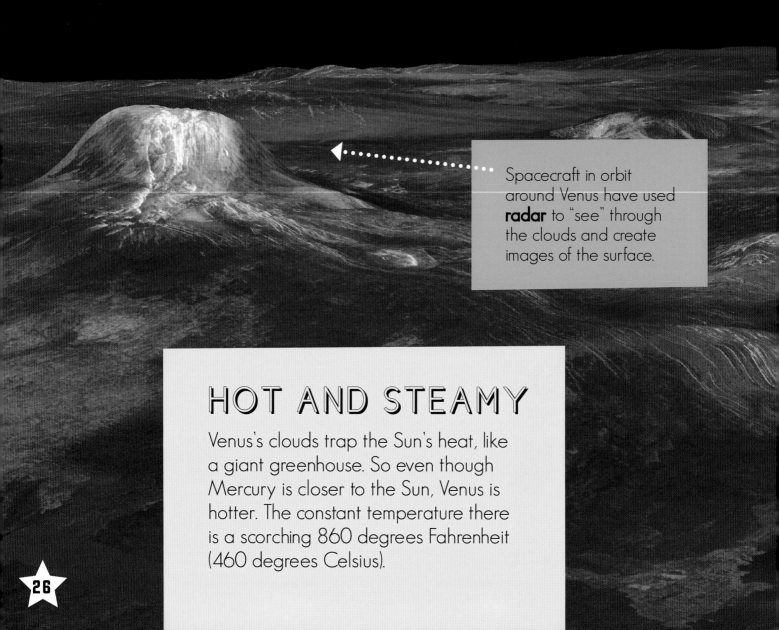

Spacecraft in orbit around Venus have used **radar** to "see" through the clouds and create images of the surface.

HOT AND STEAMY

Venus's clouds trap the Sun's heat, like a giant greenhouse. So even though Mercury is closer to the Sun, Venus is hotter. The constant temperature there is a scorching 860 degrees Fahrenheit (460 degrees Celsius).

IT'S TOXIC

The gases surrounding Earth—including the air we breathe—make up the atmosphere. Venus has an atmosphere too, but we couldn't breathe it. It is nearly all made up of **carbon dioxide**.

The *Venera 13* spacecraft managed to send back this photo of Venus's surface before being destroyed.

STAR FACT!

Scientists have sent several spacecraft to land on Venus, but none of them survived for more than two hours. The incredible heat and pressure melted and crushed them!

PLANET EARTH

Our home planet is an amazing place. It is small and rocky, with mountains and valleys, similar to Mercury, Venus, and Mars. But is also has vast oceans, lush forests, and millions of types of plants and animals.

WATER WORLD

Earth's water really sets us apart from the other planets. Some moons have water hidden below their surface, but only Earth has oceans of liquid water. It is one of the main things that makes life here possible.

Earth's water, clouds, and land give it a blue, white, and brown appearance when seen from space.

STAR FACT!

Earth's distance from the Sun puts us in what scientists call the "Goldilocks Zone." Our planet is not too hot and not too cold—the temperature is just right for supporting life!

28

Earth's surface is beautiful and diverse, with waves of water crashing into dramatic shorelines.

Just like Mercury and our Moon, Earth has craters that show where asteroids or other objects have crashed into the planet.

THE ATMOSPHERE

Earth's atmosphere helps keep the temperature fairly constant. It also provides air for us to breathe, and it is where weather happens.

INSIDE EARTH

Earth is a rocky ball made up of different layers, one inside the other. At the center is an iron core. Outside that is a layer of hot rock called the mantle, and the rocky crust sits on top of the mantle. The oceans are part of the crust.

When a volcano erupts, it spews out lava, ash, and gases.

NEW ROCK

Earth's surface changes all the time. When a volcano erupts, hot rock from the mantle comes up to the surface. Then it cools to form new rock.

MOVING AROUND

Earth's crust is broken up into large chunks called tectonic plates, which fit together like a giant jigsaw puzzle. In some places they rub against each other, and in other places they pull apart.

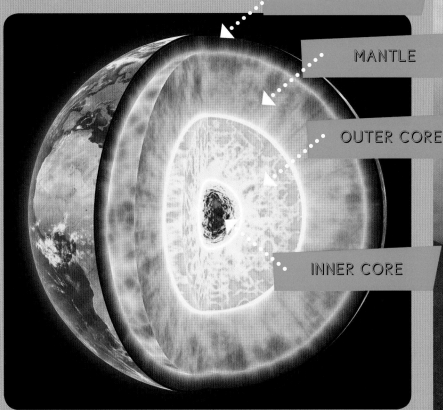

CRUST

MANTLE

OUTER CORE

INNER CORE

Earth's core is solid in the middle but liquid where it meets the mantle. The crust is a very thin layer at the top.

MARS

Traveling into space, the first planet you reach after Earth is Mars. It is just over half as wide as our home planet. It is easy to see the surface with a powerful telescope because there are no clouds to block the view.

A COLD WORLD

On average, the temperature during the day on Mars is around -58 degrees Fahrenheit (-50 degrees Celsius). In some places it can rise to 70 degrees Fahrenheit (20 degrees Celsius) or drop to -225 degrees Fahrenheit (-153 degrees Celsius).

Mars is sometimes called "the red planet" because it looks reddish from Earth. This is because its surface is rusty.

WATER ON MARS?

Mars has ice caps at each pole, just like on Earth. There is also frozen water beneath the surface. In 2015, scientists discovered that salty liquid water flows in some places on Mars!

STAR FACT!

Gravity on Mars is weaker than on Earth. If you weigh 50 pounds (23 kilograms) on Earth, you would only weigh 19 pounds (9 kilograms) on Mars!

Mars has two moons Phobos (shown here) Deimos. They are small lumpy, and covered in

The ice cap at Mars's pole is made of water and frozen carbon dio

MARS'S SURFACE

Billions of years ago, Mars was probably much warmer. It may have had rivers and oceans, just like Earth. But this liquid water is long gone, leaving behind a dry, dusty planet.

VALLEYS AND VOLCANOES

The surface of Mars is marked with deep valleys and **canyons**. It also has many volcanoes, including Olympus Mons, the biggest volcano in the solar system. It is three times higher than Mount Everest!

The *Curiosity* rover took this photo of a sandy-floored valley and a rocky outcrop in May 2015.

WEATHER ON MARS

It never rains on Mars, but sometimes small, wispy clouds form. The main weather events on Mars are dust storms. These wild winds swirl across the planet, blowing around the light dust on the surface.

This photo, taken by the *Opportunity* rover, shows the true colors of Mars's rocks and dust.

EXPLORING MARS

Humans have never visited Mars, but we have sent many spacecraft to explore it. These robotic researchers help scientists learn more about the planet. One day, astronauts may land on Mars.

The *Curiosity* rover is the size of a small car. It landed on Mars in 2012.

IN THE AIR

Spacecraft like the *Mars Global Surveyor* go into orbit around the planet. They fly around it over and over, taking photographs that help to map the planet's surface.

ON THE GROUND

Robotic rovers are spacecraft that land on a space object and drive around. Rovers have driven across the surface of Mars. Their cameras take amazing close-up photos. Their tools help scientists learn about Mars's rocks, and find out if anything lived there.

Mars Global Surveyor studied the planet for 10 years and took thousands of images.

STAR FACT!

By 2015, the *Opportunity* rover had driven the same distance as a marathon race —26 miles (42 kilometers). It took more than 11 years to get that far!

JUPITER

After Mars, the next planet is Jupiter. It is the largest planet, and it is so big that all of the other planets could fit inside it.

GAS GIANT

Jupiter is very different from the inner planets. Instead of being a rocky ball, it is mostly made of gas. That means that there is no solid surface for a spacecraft to land on.

Scientists think that Jupiter may have solid or liquid layers beneath its layers of gas.

STAR FACT!

There is a huge distance between Mars and Jupiter. In fact, Jupiter's orbit is more than three times farther from the Sun than Mars's is!

JUPITER

EARTH

Jupiter is about 11 times as wide as Earth, and more than 1,000 Earths could fit inside it.

SPINNING AROUND

Jupiter is not a very quick mover. It travels around the Sun at 8 miles (13 kilometers) per second. That might sound fast, but Mercury is almost four times faster. The one thing Jupiter does do quickly is spin on its **axis**. It takes less than 10 hours to go all the way around.

JUPITER'S CLOUDS AND STORMS

Jupiter looks stripy, with bands of yellow, brown, and white. These stripes are actually bands of clouds. Some of the bands move in opposite directions, and there are often storms where they meet.

CURIOUS CLOUDS

Clouds on Earth are made of water, but most of Jupiter's clouds are made of crystals of a smelly chemical called ammonia. Flashes of lightning there can be 1,000 times as powerful as lightning on Earth.

Some scientists think there are clouds of water beneath the top layer of ammonia clouds.

WIND

In Jupiter's storm clouds, there can be winds of up to 224 miles (360 kilometers) per hour. Storms can grow to a huge size in just a few hours.

GREAT RED SPOT

Jupiter's famous Great Red Spot is a giant storm. It has lasted for more than 400 years.

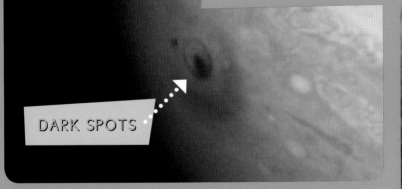

DARK SPOTS

In 1994, large chunks of a comet crashed into Jupiter, leaving dark spots on its surface.

JUPITER'S MOONS

Jupiter has more moons than any other planet—67 and counting! Four of them are large, but the rest are smaller, and have only been discovered since 2001.

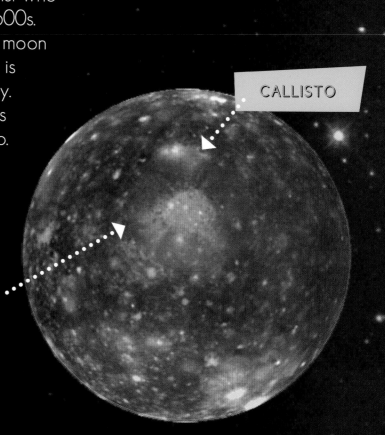

EUROPA

GALILEAN MOONS

Jupiter's four largest moons are called Galilean moons after Galileo Galilei, the scientist who discovered them in the 1600s. Ganymede is the largest moon in the solar system, and it is even bigger than Mercury. The other Galilean moons are Io, Europa, and Callisto.

CALLISTO

Jupiter's individual moon names are taken from characters in Greek mythology.

IO

STAR FACT!

Saturn is famous for its beautiful rings, but Jupiter also has rings. They are mostly made of dust, and they weren't discovered until 1979.

SMALL MOONS

Jupiter's small moons are very small indeed. Europa is 1,940 miles (3,122 kilometers) across, but the next biggest moon is less than one-tenth as big. Most of them are just 1–2 miles (1.6–3.2 kilometers) across.

GANYMEDE

Europa's surface is made of ice, criss-crossed with cracks. There may be an ocean of liquid water underneath.

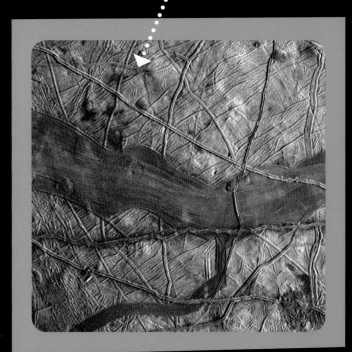

SATURN

Saturn is the next planet after Jupiter, and it is the second-biggest planet. It has yellowish stripes, a little like Jupiter, but what makes it stand out is the halo of beautiful rings that surrounds it.

HOT AND GASSY

Like Jupiter, Saturn is mostly made of gas. Its bands of clouds get their colors from the chemicals they're made of. At the planet's core, the temperature is really hot: about 21,150 degrees Fahrenheit (11,732 degrees Celsius).

Saturn is easy to find in the night sky, but you need a small telescope to see its rings.

MOVING AROUND

Saturn travels through space even more slowly than Jupiter. It takes more than 29 years to complete one orbit around the Sun. But like Jupiter, Saturn is a fast spinner. It **rotates** in just under 11 hours.

Saturn's super-fast winds, which can blow at more than 1,118 miles (1,800 kilometers) per hour, give it a stripy appearance.

The *Cassini* spacecraft started orbiting Saturn in 2004. Since then, it has sent back a lot of new information about the planet.

STAR FACT!

Saturn is huge, but because it is made of gas, it's not very dense. In fact, if you put it in water, it would float!

SATURN'S RINGS

Saturn's rings spread out in a flat disk around the center of the planet. They stretch out into space for more than 175,000 miles (282,000 kilometers), but they are very thin. Many are only about 33 feet (10 meters) thick.

TINY PIECES

The rings are made of billions of pieces of dust, rock, and ice. Some pieces are smaller than a grain of sand, and others are as big as a house.

STAR FACT!

Saturn's rings are always on the move. They circle around the planet at high speeds.

Big chunks of rock or ice could destroy a spacecraft, but *Cassini* made it safely through the rings.

Saturn's rings are divided into sections, each named with a different letter. There are gaps between the different sections.

WHERE DID THEY COME FROM?

Scientists aren't sure how the rings formed. One idea is that they are made from pieces of a moon. If the moon was destroyed by something crashing into it, the tiny pieces left behind might form rings.

MOONS OF SATURN

Saturn has 62 moons, and there are probably more still to be discovered. Some of the smaller moons are found within the rings. Their gravity helps the rings keep their shape. Many of the bigger moons are much farther out.

TITAN

Titan is Saturn's largest moon, and it is the only one we have explored. The *Huygens* spacecraft landed there on January 14, 2005, and it sent back data for more than an hour.

Huygens was the first spacecraft to land on a planet or moon in the outer solar system.

UNUSUAL MOONS

Enceladus is mostly made of ice, and it has volcanoes that shoot ice crystals into the air. Mimas has an enormous crater on one side. Iapetus is black on one side and white on the other.

STAR FACT!

Some of the ice crystals from the volcanoes on Enceladus become part of Saturn's rings!

The size of this crater on Mimas has led to the moon's nickname of the "Death Star," because it looks so much like the spaceship from *Star Wars*.

URANUS

After Saturn, there is a huge gap. The next planet is about twice as far from the Sun as Saturn is! It is Uranus, a bluish-green gas planet about one-third as wide as Jupiter.

ICY GIANT

Uranus has the coldest temperatures in the solar system. The temperature at the tops of its clouds is about -371 degrees Fahrenheit (-224 degrees Celsius). It is so cold that it is made of ice as well as gas.

Uranus gets its beautiful color from the methane in its atmosphere.

Uranus is so far away that even photos taken by the powerful Hubble Space Telescope

Other **astronomers** had seen Uranus, but they thought it was a star. William Herschel realized that it was a planet.

STAR FACT!

Uranus was the first planet to be discovered by using a telescope. William Herschel found it in 1781.

DAYS AND YEARS

A day on Uranus is shorter than a day on Earth; it lasts just over 17 hours. But a year on Uranus is much longer! Uranus takes more than 83 Earth years to complete one orbit around the Sun.

RINGS AND MOONS

All of the outer planets have rings, and that includes Uranus. They are not as big as Saturn's, but Uranus does have about 13 rings. It also has at least 27 moons.

FINDING THE RINGS

Uranus's rings were discovered in 1977. Scientists were watching Uranus pass in front of a star, when the star seemed to blink out a few times. The rings were blocking its light.

STAR FACT!

All of the moons in the solar system are named after characters in mythology, except for Uranus's moons. Most of them are named after characters in Shakespeare's plays.

Uranus's axis is tilted so much that the planet looks like it is tipped over on its side. The rings are seen at a different angle than Saturn's are.

UNUSUAL MOON

Miranda is one of the oddest moons in the solar system. It is made of rock and ice, with craters, ridges, valleys, and steep cliffs. But none of its parts seem to match up. It's a bit like a crazy patchwork quilt.

The Hubble Space Telescope orbits Earth and takes pictures of space. It has helped discover some of Uranus's moons.

NEPTUNE

Neptune is a lot like Uranus. It is slightly smaller and much farther from the Sun, but it is also blue. It is made of the same rocks, ice, and gases that make up Uranus.

COLD AND STORMY

Like Uranus, Neptune is very cold and stormy. Its winds can travel at up to 1,300 miles (2,100 kilometers) per hour! It is so far from the Sun that it takes a very long time—165 years—to go all the way around.

STAR FACT!

You couldn't stand on Neptune because there is no solid surface. But if you could, you would find that the strength of its gravity is very similar to Earth's.

RINGS AND MOONS

Neptune has five thin rings and 13 moons. The largest moon is called Triton, and all of the moons are named after sea gods.

Neptune has a white cloud called the "scooter." It changes in shape as it travels around the planet.

SCOOTER

Scientists think that Neptune's moon Triton might once have been a dwarf planet. It was captured by Neptune's gravity.

VOYAGER 2

Only one spacecraft has ever flown past Uranus and Neptune. *Voyager 2* was launched way back in 1977, and it took more than eight years to get to Uranus. It didn't reach Neptune until 1989.

MAKING DISCOVERIES

Voyager 2 also flew past Jupiter and Saturn. Before its journey, we didn't know much about the gas giants or their moons. *Voyager 2* discovered several new moons, and it sent back amazing photos of these unknown worlds.

Voyager 2 and its sister ship, *Voyager 1*, have traveled farther than anything else made by humans.

WHERE IS IT NOW?

Voyager 2 is nearing the edge of the solar system and will then travel farther out into space. It is still sending messages back to Earth. In about 40,000 years it may reach another star.

Voyager 2 launched from Cape Canaveral in Florida on August 20, 1977.

In case anyone ever finds them, the *Voyager* spacecraft carry golden discs. The discs have photos, sounds, and information about Earth.

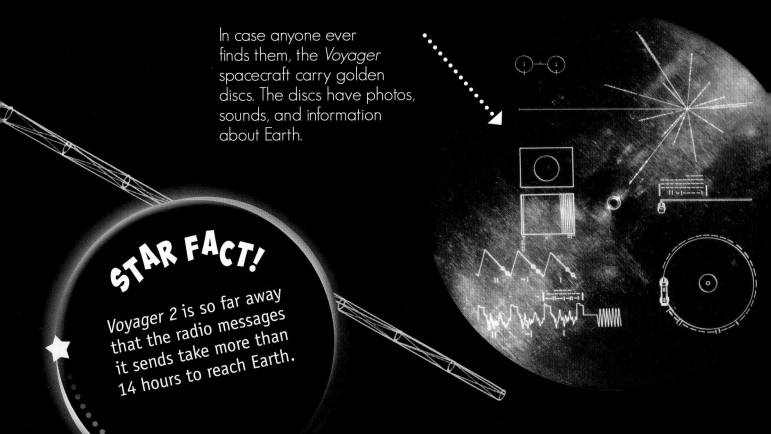

STAR FACT!

Voyager 2 is so far away that the radio messages it sends take more than 14 hours to reach Earth.

DWARF PLANETS

Until 2006, everyone thought that the solar system had nine planets. Then, a group of astronomers decided that Pluto, the ninth planet, wasn't really a planet after all. They made a new category for it—dwarf planets.

WHY CHANGE?

Astronomers had started to find a lot of objects that were about the same size as Pluto. They couldn't all be planets, could they? The astronomers realized that Pluto wasn't much like the other eight planets—it was more like these new objects.

STAR FACT!

Dwarf planets are solid and made of rock or ice. There may be over 100 dwarf planets in our solar system. Some of them have their own moons!

Past Neptune is the Kuiper Belt, a huge group of small, icy objects, including some dwarf planets. From this far out, the sun looks like a bright star.

Most dwarf planets are found out past Neptune, but Ceres is between Mars and Jupiter.

DWARF RULES

A dwarf planet has to be round, like a ball. It has to travel around the Sun, and not around another planet. All dwarf planets are much smaller than the eight main planets—even smaller than Earth's Moon.

PLUTO

Pluto was discovered in 1930, by Clyde Tombaugh. Pluto is a cold, rocky ball about half as wide as Mercury. It was called the "ninth planet" for 76 years, until it was demoted to dwarf planet.

These newly-discovered mountains are about 0.5–1 mile (1–1.5 kilometers) high.

INSIDE PLUTO

Scientists think that Pluto has a rocky core at its center, surrounded by a thick layer of ice. The top surface is made of frozen nitrogen. The surface has many flat areas, as well as mountains up to 11,000 feet (3,500 meters) high.

NEW HORIZONS

The *New Horizons* spacecraft flew past Pluto in 2015. It was the first spacecraft to visit the planet. It took the first-ever clear photographs of Pluto and its moons.

New Horizons showed us for the first time that Pluto's surface had bright, icy plains and darker cratered areas.

Pluto's largest moon, Charon, is about half as wide as Pluto. The other four moons are much smaller.

THE ASTEROID BELT

There is more to our solar system than just planets. Millions of smaller objects, such as asteroids, also orbit the Sun. Most of the asteroids are found in a "belt" between the orbits of Mars and Jupiter.

LEFTOVERS

When the solar system first formed, there were a lot of chunks of rock flying around. Some chunks collided and stuck together, getting bigger until they formed planets or moons. Asteroids are the leftovers that never grew big enough.

Movies show asteroids as being close together, but most are at least 621,000 miles (1,000,000 kilometers) apart.

STAR FACT!

The NEAR Shoemaker spacecraft landed on an asteroid called Eros. Another spacecraft actually brought rock samples from an asteroid back to Earth!

Asteroids sometimes crash into Earth, leaving huge craters like this one, named Shoemaker in Western Australia.

SMALL AND LUMPY

Most asteroids are lumpy and oddly shaped, and covered in craters. Only the biggest ones are close to being round. Even though they are so small, some asteroids have their own moons: smaller asteroids that orbit them.

VESTA

Vesta was discovered more than 200 years ago, and it is the second-largest asteroid found so far. We know a lot about Vesta because the *Dawn* spacecraft orbited it for about a year, from 2011-2012.

SIZE AND CRATERS

Vesta is about 326 miles (525 kilometers) wide—less than one-sixth the size of our Moon. Its rocky surface is covered with craters. Long ago, large objects crashed into it, sending some of its rock flying off into space.

STAR FACT!

Two objects in the asteroid belt are bigger than Vesta: Ceres and Pallas. Ceres is now called a dwarf planet.

This photo shows Vesta's north pole, which was still in darkness when *Dawn* first arrived.

MOTHER OF METEORITES

Scientists are pretty sure that many of the **meteorites** that land on Earth are pieces of Vesta. The types of rock in the meteorites match what *Dawn* learned about the rocks on Vesta.

Vesta is not really brightly colored, but in this close-up of one of its craters, the different colors represent different types of rock.

COMETS

Every so often, our planet sees a visitor from the outer solar system. Comets are icy lumps with long, beautiful tails streaming out behind them. Some of them can appear in the sky for days or weeks.

Every so often a bright comet passes close enough to Earth to make a spectacular show in the sky.

AROUND THE SUN

Most comets come from the farthest parts of the solar system. They travel in long, looping paths around the Sun before heading back where they came from. Sometimes we can see them from Earth as they pass by.

Comet sightings are fairly rare. Donati's Comet was first documented in 1858 but won't fly by Earth again until after the year 4000.

A BAD OMEN?

Long ago, many people were scared of comets. They didn't understand what they were, and when a comet appeared in the sky, they thought it was a sign that something bad would happen soon.

COMET TAILS

Comets are mostly made of ice and dust, and when they get close to the Sun, the ice starts to heat up and turn into gas. As the comet travels, the gas and dust stream out to form a tail.

During Comet Hale-Bopp's journey past Earth in 1997, you could clearly see the brownish-white dust tail (at the bottom) and the blue gas tail (at the top).

TWO TAILS

Most comets have two tails. One is made of dust, similar to the smoke from a fire. The other is made of gas. The gas tail usually looks blue and straight, while the dust tail is more curved and brownish.

STAR FACT!

Each time a comet goes around the Sun, it gets a bit smaller. This is because some of its ice and dust are left behind as a tail.

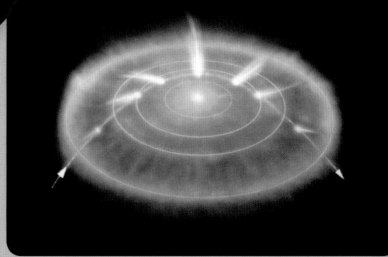

This diagram shows a comet's path around the Sun. When it is moving toward the Sun, its tail streams out behind it. But when it is moving away from the Sun, its tail is pushed out in front of it.

MOVING AWAY

When you ride your bike fast, your hair blows out behind you. But a comet is different: no matter which way it is going, its tails always point away from the sun.

ROSETTA AND PHILAE

On November 12, 2014, history was made when a spacecraft the size of a washing machine bounced across the surface of an icy, rocky lump. It was *Philae*, the first spacecraft ever to land safely on a comet.

STAR FACT!

Rosetta and *Philae* were launched in 2004. It took them more than 10 years to reach the comet.

TWO-PART MISSION

Philae was part of a spacecraft called *Rosetta*, and their target was a comet called 67P. When they got there, *Rosetta* went into orbit around the comet and dropped *Philae* onto the surface.

Rosetta is the first spacecraft to go into orbit around a comet. Its job is to study the comet and relay *Philae*'s signals to Earth.

SOURCE OF LIFE?

When Earth was first formed, many comets crashed into it. Scientists think that the original building blocks of life came from these comets. *Philae* found chemicals that support this idea.

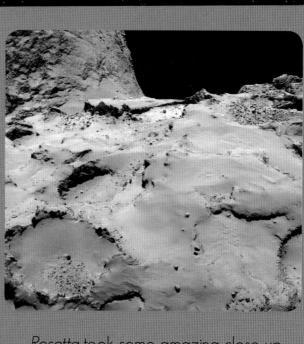

Rosetta took some amazing close-up photos of the comet's surface. These helped astronomers choose a good landing site for *Philae*.

METEORS

Some nights, if you are lucky, you may see a tiny point of light streak across the sky. We call it a shooting star, but it's not really a star. It's a small piece of rock burning up as it flies through Earth's atmosphere.

In 2013, a huge meteor in Russia caused a fireball to streak across the sky.

TINY BUT BRIGHT

Most of the **meteors** we see are space rocks no bigger than a pebble. They burn up completely and never hit the ground. Sometimes bigger objects don't burn up completely, and what's left lands on Earth.

DIFFERENT NAMES

In space there are many small rocks called meteoroids. When one falls through a planet's atmosphere and starts to glow, it is called a meteor. If part of it survives the trip and lands on the surface, the rock is called a meteorite.

Sometimes a lot of meteors happen together. This is called a meteor shower, and it happens when Earth passes through the tail of a comet.

STAR FACT!

Meteoroids travel incredibly fast. Their speed when they enter the atmosphere can be up to 45 miles (72 kilometers) per second.

METEORITES

Meteorites are pretty amazing objects: rocks from space that land on our doorstep! They give scientists clues about what other planets and objects are made of.

METAL AND STONE

Not all meteorites are the same. Some are made of rock, some are made of metal, and some are a mixture of rock and metal. Most of the ones that fall to Earth are the stone type.

Antarctica is a great place to find meteorites. They are easy to spot against the ice and snow.

STAR FACT!

Scientists estimate that nearly 50 tons (45 tonnes) of rock from space lands on Earth each day.

WHERE DO THEY COME FROM?

Sometimes scientists can tell where meteorites come from, based on what they are made of. Nearly all meteorites come from asteroids, but a few come from Mars or the Moon.

This massive piece of iron in Africa is the largest meteorite ever found. It weighs about 66 tons (60 tonnes).

OUR PLACE IN THE UNIVERSE

Our solar system is big, but it is just a tiny part of the universe. Stars are clumped together in giant groups called **galaxies**. Our Sun is one of hundreds of billions of stars in a galaxy called the Milky Way.

Our solar system is located in a part of the Milky Way called the Orion arm.

MANY GALAXIES

It's hard to picture just how big the Milky Way is, but there are many more galaxies out there, each with billions of stars. Astronomers think there are more than 100 billion galaxies in the universe.

STAR FACT!

After the Sun, our closest star is Proxima Centauri. Even if you could travel at the speed of light, it would take more than four years to get there.

On a really dark night, you can see the white band of the Milky Way streaming across the sky.

THE SUN

WHAT'S OUT THERE?

Many of the stars in distant galaxies have planets traveling around them. Some of those planets have their own moons. It's possible that somewhere out there is another planet with life, like ours.

Astronomers have found more than 2,000 planets orbiting other stars. Some are gas giants, and others are small and rocky, like Earth.

asteroid a small, rocky body that orbits the Sun and is smaller than a planet or dwarf planet

astronomer a person who studies planets, stars, and other objects in space

atmosphere the layer of gases surrounding a planet, moon, or star

atom the smallest possible unit of matter

axis an imaginary line through the center of a planet, around which it rotates

canyon a narrow valley with steep sides, often with a stream or river flowing through it

carbon dioxide a gas that we breathe out. It is found in Earth's atmosphere and other places in space.

comet an icy object in space that travels in a long looping path around the Sun. Comets usually form a long, bright tail as they move through the sky.

core the center area of something, such as a planet

coronal mass ejection a huge bubble of gas and magnetism released by the Sun over a period of a few hours

crater a hollow area, like the inside of a bowl, created when an object crashes into a planet or other large object

dwarf planet an object in the solar system that is not big enough, or does not have strong enough gravity, to be considered a planet

eclipse the blocking out of one object by another, for example when the Moon blocks out the Sun

energy the ability to do work

galaxy a group of billions of stars and other objects held together by gravity

gravity the force that pulls all objects towards each other

lava molten rock that comes out of a volcano

magnetic field the space around a magnet in which a magnetic force is active

mass a measure of how much matter is in an object

matter the substance that makes up any object or material

meteor a red-hot meteoroid traveling through Earth's atmosphere, visible as a bright streak across the sky

meteorite a lump of stone or metal from space that has landed on Earth

meteoroid a small lump of rock or other matter that travels through the solar system. Meteoroids sometimes enter Earth's atmosphere, becoming meteors.

moon an object that orbits a planet, dwarf planet, or asteroid

orbit to travel around another object in a curved path. The planets in our solar sytem orbit the Sun.

planet a large object that orbits a star, with nothing else in its path

radar the use of radio waves to study faraway objects. Waves are sent out and then picked up again when they bounce back after hitting an object.

rotate to spin around a central axis. The rotation of our Earth is what causes night and day.

rover a robot vehicle that travels across the surface of a planet or moon and collects data

solar system a sun and everything in orbit around it, such as planets, asteroids, and comets

star an enormous ball of hot glowing gas

telescope a tool that makes faraway things look closer

trillion a million million

volcano a mountain with a hole in the top or side that can send out rocks, ash, lava, and gas in an eruption

INDEX